THE STORY OF MUSIC IN CARTOON

BERNARD DYRIES   **DENYS LEMERY**

Translated by Michael Sadler

THE STORY OF MUSIC IN CARTOON

FROM PRE-HISTORY TO THE PRESENT

MACDONALD & CO
LONDON & SYDNEY

Dear Reader (or 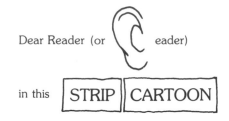 eader)

in this | STRIP | CARTOON |

you'll find a lot of

P I C T U R E S

but very little **TEXT TEXT TEXT**

What we hope to provide are some

musical

F O U N D A T I O N S

If you long to know more

(me

music)   then you

would do well to consult

Only problem . . . This book contains a lot of

T E   X T

but very few

Pictures

A Macdonald Book

First published in Great Britain in 1983
by Macdonald & Co (Publishers) Ltd, London Sydney.

Copyright © 1978 Editions Francis Van de Velde,
        12, rue Jacob, 75006 Paris
Copyright for this translation © 1983 Arco Publications Inc.

Macdonald & Co
London & Sydney
Maxwell House
74 Worship Street
London EC2A 2EN

ISBN 0 356 09409 X

Printed in Belgium by H. Proost & Cie.

The story of music begins with the story of man...

To fend for himself, Stone Age man invents tools for digging and weapons for hunting. The first "musical" instruments come into being.

A hollow branch or an old bone makes a flute, a stretched skin a drum, a bowstring a guitar string.

Primitive man hears Nature's call...

...Which he copies...

And so music is born.

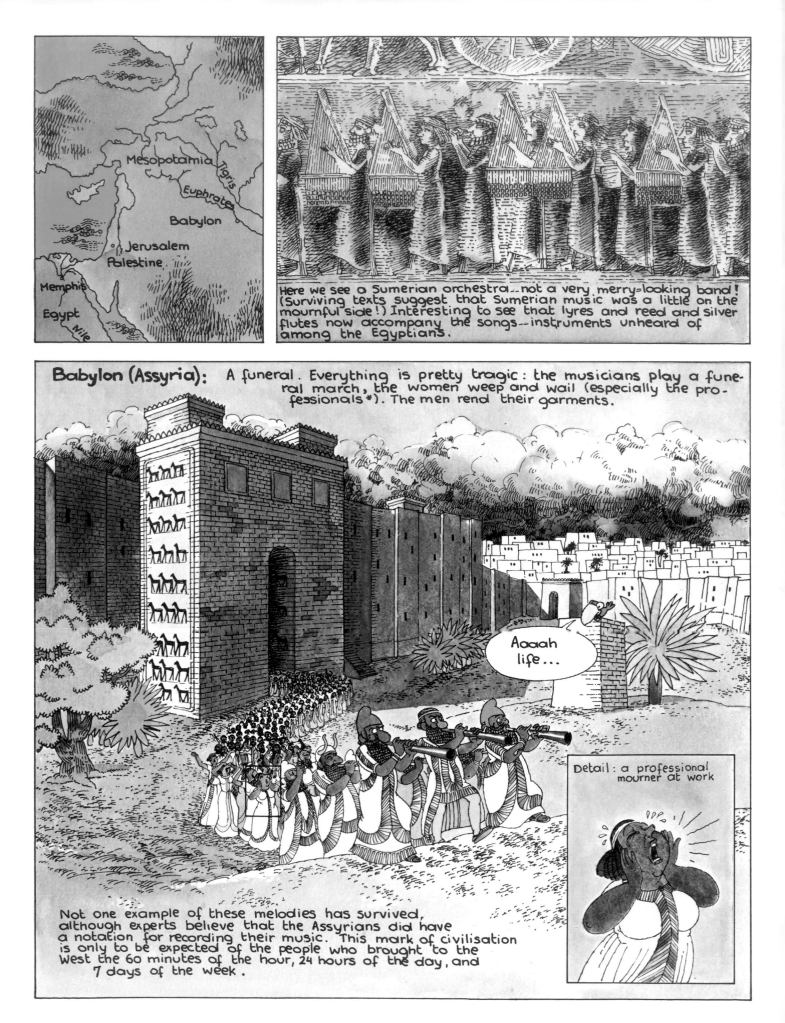

Here we see a Sumerian orchestra...not a very merry-looking band! (Surviving texts suggest that Sumerian music was a little on the mournful side!) Interesting to see that lyres and reed and silver flutes now accompany the songs—instruments unheard of among the Egyptians.

Babylon (Assyria): A funeral. Everything is pretty tragic: the musicians play a funeral march, the women weep and wail (especially the professionals *). The men rend their garments.

Aaaah life...

Detail: a professional mourner at work

Not one example of these melodies has survived, although experts believe that the Assyrians did have a notation for recording their music. This mark of civilisation is only to be expected of the people who brought to the West the 60 minutes of the hour, 24 hours of the day, and 7 days of the week.

About 1000 BC: The Hebrew Court. Without any doubt King David is the greatest composer and poet of his age. Music is so important to him that his court includes a choir of 300 -- who sing psalms* to the accompaniment of harps, lyres, cymbals and over a hundred trumpets!

*religious songs

Some 300 years later... With the disappearance of the Hebrew Kingdom of Israel, music becomes a little less solemn. Drums and citharas accompany the teachings of the prophets.

Later still... in Greece, or to be more exact, on Mount Olympus... we find Zeus, the King of the Gods, who rules (ok), but not without the odd headache. Gods tend to be undisciplined, but a few are musical. The patron of music is Apollo (here in his chariot)--helped by a muse* Pan plays on his pipes--a flute made from reeds of varying length -- invented by Pan in memory of the nymph Syrinx. He wanted to kiss her, but she turned into a reed! Mercury is a little flighty--and has a penchant for the dance!

*Hence "music".

Zeus's thunderbolt

Legend has it that when Zeus wanted to make himself heard he used his thunderbolt to tell the mythical musicians to put a sock in it.

Mr. Pan, you're simply divine...

Greek legend provides many examples of the magical powers of music... Orpheus's singing -- to the sound of his lyre -- bewitches Charon, the keeper of Hell, into letting him slip by to his beloved Eurydice.

The Greeks go on the warpath to the sound of music! It boosts their confidence.
All the armies of the world will later follow their example.

Between wars the Greeks build those masterpieces of architecture whose ruins are now one of the tourist wonders of the world. Their civilisation will exert a long and lasting influence on the West.

Meantime ... in Ancient Gaul, Celtic bards sing epic songs about the exploits of Great Warriors.

The Roman Empire crumbles under the Barbarian invasion from the East. War and folklore once again encourage song-making— but now of a Barbarian kind! Their most famous legend tells of the Nibelungen.[1] This vast Scandinavian and Germanic epic (or Lied) will—much later—inspire Richard Wagner.[2]

[2) see page 77

feuer[3] ...

[1] The Nibelungen-lied is to the Barbarians what the Iliad and Odyssey were to the Greeks!

[3] Fire ...

The last 300 years have been a turbulent period. Wars and invasions have held up the advance of civilisation—and of music! Peace (at last) returns around the year 800. The Catholic Church is now all-powerful and authority is in the hands of the kings.

Charlemagne is the most powerful ruler in Europe. Under him, the Gregorian Chant becomes more widely used—even though Pope Gregory had ordered all churches to use it some two centuries earlier!

de us miseric
diunit

Gregorian chants are written down by the monks, the only people who can read and write. This is why we know something of church music, but little of mediaeval "pop".

Gregorian chants are for the voice alone. Accompaniment involves using "instruments of the devil"—according to St. Aloysius!

Up until the Middle Ages music is based on one melodic line. During the Middle Ages things get more complicated -- with the arrival of polyphony. This is the art of combining several different melodic lines, all based on one tune. At first people found the results a little surprising ...

Religious music is very austere. To the church's horror... a new kind of music appears: popular music!

Thanks to the Great Crusades of the Middle Ages, musicians find an audience outside the church.
These long holy journeys also enrich their repertory of songs ...

And so the profession of composer is born.

Meanwhile... back in the country

... Agriculture is looking up, thanks to newly developed techniques. Famines happen less often. And trade gets off the ground... with people peddling not only their wares, but their artistic and musical skills too.

This is the age of the troubadour and the minstrel.

A minstrel is of lowly birth, a troubadour noble...
But both are essentially musicians. They travel from
castle to castle entertaining knights and noblemen
with songs of gallantry: in war, in crusades and
in love!

Doubtless the most famous
troubadour of them all is...a
king of England: Richard the
Lion-Hearted.

Popular music joins forces with church music in
the mystery plays, which are acted on the very
doorsteps of the cathedrals.

**The whole of Europe bursts
into song...**
In Germany the Minnesinger
warble the beauties of nature.

Pilgrims in Spain sing hymns
on their travels.

Franciscan monks in Italy
sing of their love of animals.

Around 1300, Philippe de Vitry, Bishop of Meaux (France), writes a book on new techniques of musical composition: the "Ars Nova" ("The New Art").

The first important work of Ars Nova is "Le Roman de Fauvel"—a work written and performed by a group of musicians.

The "Roman de Fauvel" is a satire of society. Thanks to Dame Fortune, the donkey Fauvel is crowned king... But—to keep their privileges—noblemen and clergy happily pay homage to a donkey! A tournament is arranged, pitting right against wrong—but nobody wins!

Once again war breaks out—this time between England and France. And this time for the next 100 years. Once again the countryside is wracked by famine and plague...

Au fou!¹

Obviously music will not flourish in a period of discord. But the musicians who follow the armies learn both from their travels... and from their enemies.

Parlez-vous français?

No, but I've got a lovely voice!

1) Fire!

b.deyus.

22

Guillaume de Machaut is one of these wandering musicians. He follows the call of battle all across Europe as part of the King of Bohemia's retinue. He composes on the move not only "rondeaux" and ballads, but also the first church mass. Pupils gather around him wherever he stops.

An Italian—Francesco Landini—is extraordinarily talented. Although blind, he can play all musical instruments with ease and excels in astronomy and philosophy! But his compositions are his real claim to fame. His music brings welcome flexibility and charm to the Ars Nova.

Machaut and Landini have many pupils, but they tend to compose in an overcomplicated style. Music goes through the doldrums... until the first English victory of the Hundred Years War.
1415: Agincourt.

English composers—although originally taught by the School of Notre Dame—quickly turn their backs on the high-falutin' complexities of Ars Nova... and devote themselves to melody.
Music gets a new lease on life. And the influence of the English spreads to their allies in Burgundy and Flanders.

25

Signs of the Renaissance are every-where to be seen—as much in everyday life as in the arts. Castles, which had been closed and barricaded in times of war, are now transformed for a more open, agreeable life...

Kings and princes now try to outshine (not kill!) each other—and gather around them glittering courts, made up of painters, poets and musicians. Francis I of France leads the field, attracting the most brilliant artists of his time.

Nom d'un chien, what a dazzling court, François.

Don't look now, but there's a dazzling artist trying to dazzle you, Duchess.

1515... 1515... Somehow that rings a bell...

... exquisite gardens are planted... Horticulture and courtship develop hand in hand...

"The Hunt"

"The Cries of Paris"

The French composer Clement Jannequin sets himself the task of making music from the sounds of everyday life. His songs include "The Hunt", "The Cries of Paris", "The Gossips" and even the famous "Battle of Marignan", in which singers imitate the sounds of battle.

cluck, cluck...
cluck...cluck...
cluck..cluck..
cluck, cluck..
cluck..cluck..

"The Gossips"

Jannequin's songs are famous all over Europe. Musicians are soon influenced by his freedom of expression: e.g., the Flemish/Italian Adrian Willaert, who invents the madrigal (p.26), or the Frenchman, Roland de Lassus, for whose story... please turn over.

CRUMP BOOOMM
BANG! BANG!
CLIPPETY SPLASH CLIPPETY

"The Battle of Marignan"

27

One day, while journeying through Flanders, the Viceroy of Sicily stumbles upon a 12-year-old boy with a beautiful voice and decides to take him along. This young lad is Roland de Lassus.

The young Roland learns his music on his many travels with his master.

In later life he will continue to travel: Italy, England, Germany (where he spends many years as choirmaster in Munich*). His fame is immense... as is the number of his compositions... over 2400 works! (More than those of Bach and Mozart combined!!) His music reflects all the styles of the period. De Lassus is the ultimate European musician!

* All musicians before the 18th century will cast longing eyes at the title of "Choirmaster"... since it allows reasonable freedom to compose... and helps keep the wolf from the door!

Italy and Germany are now both a jigsaw of tiny independent states. When not fighting among themselves they try to out-dazzle each other's courts and... of course... their artists! Musicians, competing to be the most original, turn to the local popular music for inspiration. Hence, the "Italian style", the "French style", the "English style" etc...

1536: Another Italian boy wonder...Palestrina...has a beautiful voice. At the age of 11 his parents put him in the custody of the Pope...to be part of the Papal choir.

Giovanni PALESTRINA
furs and leather

As choirmaster of the Sistine Chapel, Palestrina will work under no less than eleven Popes! He works alongside his second wife in the skintrade...she is the widow of a rich fur merchant attached to the Papal court -- but still finds time to compose ... 115 masses, more than 100 motets, countless madrigals, hymns, psalms, canticles, etc...

A madrigal is a love song based on a popular tune, but with a very skilful musical structure. Luca Marenzio uses this kind of music to the full...as does Orenzio Vecchi. One of his "madrigal operas" is being performed opposite. It involves lots of characters and an incredibly complicated plot...

LOVE

... In fact, I can't make beak or tail of what's going on... they all look feather-brained to me!

29

In England things look rosier. The reigns of Henry VII, Mary Tudor and Elizabeth I see the conquest of America and the beginnings of trade with the Indies. The economy flourishes. So do the arts.

Music is still, apart from popular songs, only for the privileged nobility and clergy. Henry VIII—here seen executing (a courtly air)—was a remarkable musician and his court a centre of musical activity.

This is also the age of the great poet and dramatist William Shakespeare. Music has an important part in his plays (Ophelia's dying song in "Hamlet", the musical interludes used to bring King Lear back to his senses, etc...)

These 16th-century musicians compose for the viols (string instruments played with a bow), the lute and the virginal (a keyboard instrument belonging to the harpsichord family).

music in Shakespeare's England

tallis
gibbons
dowland
william byrd

Spain under Philip II tries to overwhelm the English by its military strength. But, in 1588, the "invincible" Armada meets its match...and Drake, after bowls!

At the King's court in Madrid the music of Tomás Luis de Victoria is truly Spanish—even if that of Morales or Antonio de Cabezón is much influenced by their French and Italian fellow-musicians.

Fire!

Honest? Maybe not. But musical? Oh, boy...

HASSLER
metal
goods
and music

Germany is a deeply divided country during this period and musicians make little mark. Except perhaps for Hassler—a student of de Lassus and the Gabrieli—who tries to merge polyphony with the style of the Venetian School. In business Hassler is said to be more artful than artistic!

The monk Martin Luther (who started the Reformation) promotes the use of the Chorale in all the "new" churches.

Luther loves music, and is sure that the most beautiful music imaginable must be pleasing to God.

But two new musical forms are developed in Germany: the LIED (a poem set to music), used later to such effect by Schubert; and, more important still, the CHORALE, which sets religious words to popular music.

It is Johann Sebastian Bach who will eventually perfect the Chorale. In the meantime Luther and the Reformation give German music a much needed shot in the arm.

See p. 56

These two dance scenes—one peasant, one aristocratic—remind us that, up till now, musical instruments have been used purely for accompaniment.

Towards the end of the 16th century, new instruments are making themselves heard and their "families" get ever larger! At this concert below, a virginal is accompanied by:

1. lute
2. orpharion (cittern)
3. chitarrone
4. drum and tambourine
5. virginal
6. viola de Gamba
7. courtaut (double reed)
8. violin
9. trombone
10. harp
11. bass recorder
12. crumhorn

The German composer Praetorius is one of the first to see the value of musical instruments in themselves. In fact, he composes only instrumental works. In the early 17th century he publishes a vast treatise where he develops his theories about instruments and musical structures.

But once again back in Italy... Let's have a peek into the palace of the Duke of Mantua (Vincent de Gonzaga to his friends).

The Duke is a real original. Patron of the arts and part-time alchemist, he is both mean and violent... He never (or hardly ever) pays his artists. He is, however, instrumental in making them famous.

For instance...and on closer inspection...

Second floor: Here we discover none other than Rubens working on his portrait of the poet Tasso.

First floor: Claudio Monteverdi, the greatest Italian musician of the century, is introducing the Duchess to his latest composition.

Meanwhile ... in the basement: the Duke is getting steamed up trying to turn lead into gold.

Tasso must be off his rocker! He thinks he's Godfrey de Bouillon!!!

The legend of Orpheus and Eurydice — of which we have already heard — is very popular among composers. Monteverdi is one of the first musicians to turn it into an opera: "Orfeo" ("Orpheus"; 1607) — the first lyric drama worthy of the name — is a signpost in the history of music.

On the Duke of Mantua's death, Monteverdi becomes choirmaster at Venice. Here he writes his first religious works, as well as madrigals and operas: "The Coronation of Poppea", "The Combat of Tancred and Clorinda" (based on a poem by his friend Tasso, floor 2 opposite).

"The Combat of Tancred and Clorinda" tells the tragic story of a Crusader and an Amazon disguised as a knight... At its first performance the audience was reduced to silence... too moved even to applaud.

Monteverdi died in Venice, a composer loved and respected by all. Sadly, not all of his works have survived. But he stands unrivalled as the Father of the Opera.

Heinrich Schütz, the son of an innkeeper from the Black Forest, studied in Venice under the Gabrieli.

❉

On returning to Germany, Schütz found a post as organist. His compositions are basically religious and for the voice.

His best known work? The Psalms of David for choir and orchestra...

Help! Fire!

The outbreak of the Thirty Years War brings with it the collapse of many small German states. Musicians are forced to lay down their instruments and to take up arms.

Musicians are scarce, so Schütz composes for smaller ensembles...

Eventually he becomes a composer at the Danish court, returning to Germany only at the end of his life. His works include psalms, passions, religious concertos, madrigals – and a beautiful Christmas oratorio.

France 1643: The young Jean-Baptiste Lully arrives in France as a kitchen boy, or so legend has it. At the age of 11 we find him at the Court of Versailles — teaching Italian to "la grande mademoiselle" — the Duchess of Montpensier.

While learning the viol and studying the art of composition, Lully makes friends with the young King Louis XIV — and teaches him some new (and fancy) dance steps...

Lully is one of the King's favourite favourites. And his music is played as often as possible. His contemporaries don't get much of a look in... One of the unfortunates is Nicolas Campra. Another is Michel Delalande, one of the greatest of the Versailles School. His major works, besides a Te Deum and a Magnificat — include a series of fanfares to be "served" at the Sun King's lavish suppers.

Delalande   Charpentier   Couperin

The only musician to escape the over-powering presence of Lully was Marc-Antoine Charpentier — probably because he managed to outlive him by 17 years! Charpentier worked with the playwright Molière — and also composed a series of stirring triumphal works, such as the Te Deum...

...part of which became the TV Eurovision theme.

But Lully remains the outstanding personality of the period. His "reign" — as personal composer to the King and director of music in his theatres — lasts all of 16 years.
Lully also worked with Molière — arranging the dance sequences for his "comédies-ballets", such as "Le Bourgeois Gentilhomme". Lully always used a big stick to beat time, and while conducting his Te Deum he missed the beat ... hit his foot... and later died from the wound.

37

Mean (mumble) while ... in... slurp... Franchhe... *

...at the time of La Fontaine and his fables (such as the crow and the fox)...

The end of the 17th century sees the setting of the Sun king's reign... and the last of the extravaganzas at Versailles... "Melancholy invades court and castle.

François Couperin is born into this weary world in 1698. Later he is to be acknowledged as supreme master of the French harpsichord school...a virtuoso of both harpsichord and organ, and composer of many pieces for both instruments.

* Moral: NEVER speak with your mouth full.

Hush, please, for Couperin's "Leçons des ténèbres".

At the start of the 18th century there is a feud between the rival supporters of French and Italian music...to be remembered as the "Quarrel of the Clowns". Whereas the likes of Voltaire and Rameau swear by French opera, others, such as Jean-Jacques Rousseau, opt for the Italians. Even the royal couple threaten to come to blows!... with a pro-Italian Queen and a (surprise surprise!) pro-French King!

"LES INDES GALANTES" A "savage" courting couple.

The "Grandmaster" of French opera is Jean-Philippe Rameau.

As well as being an important musical theorist, Rameau writes 32 operas, including "Castor and Pollux", "Hippolyte and Aricie" and above all "Les Indes Galantes". He also composes for the harpsichord. In his concert pieces, instruments play solo parts for the first time in their history.

The multitude of small states--into which Germany and Austria are divided--are often ruled by musical princes. At their sumptuous court receptions, the highlight of the evening would be... an Italian opera.

It is in Southern--Catholic--Germany that a new school of music begins to emerge - the (first) Viennese school, with Pachelbel and the famous violinist Biber.

Let's all now lend a rustic ear to Biber's "Peasants' Procession".

But there's more resistance to this Italian invasion in the Protestant North. The celebrated organist Buxtehude (born a Dane) settles at Lubeck and has the brainwave of organising the first concerts for a paying public: "Music in the evening".

His fame is such that Johann Sebastian Bach--at the age of 20--will travel nearly 200 miles on foot to hear him play.

When the city of Venice stages an opera, money is no object.

The tremendous skill of the Italian instrument makers partly explains the growth of instrumental music... and the emergence of the concerto form* Antonio Stradivari (a pupil of Amati) is the champion craftsman. The secret of his "wonderful sound" lies... (ssshh...)... in the mixing of his varnish.

What's in your varnish, Mister?

Oh, that Corelli...

Oh, that Marcello...

Oh, that Torelli...

Oh, that ravioli...

A concerto lets a soloist--backed by an orchestra--show off all his skill. Vivaldi will excel in this field. Torelli and Corelli started the "concerto grosso", where a small group of instruments converse with a bigger group.

*A concerto is a composition which allows one or more instrumental soloists to carry on a conversation with the orchestra.

Vivaldi's works are full of the music of the carnival and of Venice itself. They are light-hearted, witty and full of sunshine. His elaborate operas are equally enchanting...

A priest, Vivaldi teaches the violin to the young ladies of a Venetian religious orphanage. Some of them form an excellent orchestra, which Vivaldi is here conducting -- with **feeling**!

Vivaldi is the father of the concerto... with 600 of them... the best known being "The Four Seasons"

Nicknamed the red-headed priest, Vivaldi is much admired by his contemporaries. Bach is so impressed by him that he transcribes several of his works for the harpsichord and organ.

In 1685 in Halle, Germany, there begins an extraordinary story... for George Frederick Handel is no ordinary child...

At the age of 8 he is already an accomplished organist. Bored by his law studies, he leaves for Italy and devotes himself to music. Success arrives—but he decides to return to Germany, and the Elector of Hanover appoints him choirmaster.

Handel then begs leave to travel to England—never to return! After the success of his opera "Rinaldo" all London is at his feet.

But... in 1714 the Elector of Hanover he had deserted becomes... King of England! Handel, though famous, is in a tricky position. But he wins his way back into favour by dedicating the exuberant "Water Music" to the King.

Handel works hard and fast... the "Messiah" is completed in three weeks... about the time it takes a music copyist to transcribe the score!

He composes a vast amount: 40 operas, some 30 oratorios, organ concertos (which he plays during the intervals in the oratorios), concerti grossi, Te Deum ... phew!

His "open-air" music is among his finest: the "Water Music" and the "Music for the Royal Fireworks".

43

The German family Bach (not Swiss Family Robinson!) forms a whole musical dynasty from the 16th to the 18th centuries. The most famous member of the clan is... Johann Sebastian.

What about me!

Born in 1685 (like Handel), an orphan at 10, Bach works day and night at the music which he loves. His extraordinary gifts soon show themselves, both in his studies and his playing (on harpsichord and organ). French music is his great love.

His technical virtuosity is so great that the other competitors in an organ competition give up in despair...

I'm going to be a postman...

Johann Sebastian is attached to the court of several German princes. It is the Prince de Coethen who best recognises his gifts. While in his service Bach writes his instrumental masterpiece, the Brandenburg Concertos.

After the death of his first wife Maria Barbara (who gave him 7 children), Bach marries again -- the young singer Anna Magdalena -- who will give him 13 more!

When 38, Bach becomes "cantor" of St. Thomas in Leipzig. His very demanding contract obliges him to write a new work for each religious service. So he writes (as well as other compositions) 300 cantatas -- for each Sunday of his appointment.

But this is not all. Bach must also give part of his time to teaching. His pupils are of mixed ages... and abilities.

In spite of all these duties Bach still finds time to play in the famous Brasserie Zimmerman--alongside his better pupils.

Not the easiest task in the world--to compose oratorios, fugues and concertos... surrounded by twenty children.

Oh! Bach... I thought you said bark!!

You mean it's like this every day?!

Towards the end of his life, Bach is deeply moved by the welcome he receives from King Frederick II of Prussia in Potsdam. During a concert at the court, the king--himself an excellent flautist--invites the ageing master to accompany him.

Bach died in 1750. His fame during his lifetime was mainly as a performer. His genius as a composer was not recognised until long after his death. He wrote an enormous amount: masses, passions, cantatas, concertos, sonatas. But the musical form in which he excels is the fugue*.

* In a fugue a theme and a succession of imitations of this theme seem either to chase or to run away from each other!

45

Alive and well and living in Hamburg is a friend and contemporary of Bach who was strongly influenced by the music of Lully and of Campra. Georg Philipp Telemann composes in all the genres. His work combines the different musical currents of the period.

Telemann's operas are sparkling and sophisticated without ever being superficial. The orchestra becomes an actor in his music dramas. In "Don Quixote", a solo instrument replaces the human voice.

Three of Bach's sons are excellent musicians -- Carl Philipp Emanuel, who was Telemann's godson; Wilhelm Friedemann and Johann Christian. Their music is a bridge between the world of their father and the pre-romantic school of Haydn and Mozart.

The symphony is becoming an important musical form--thanks to Boccherini and Sammartini in Italy, and especially to Stamitz in Germany. The actual structure of the symphony is determined by the Mannheim school. Orchestras now begin to look for the finer points of interpretation.

Thanks to my Electric Thrillometer, I can record the swoon-level of the public exposed to the ravishing delights of the orchestra.

Germany and Austria are the musical centres of Europe in the last years of the 18th century. Economic change affects society, and musicians find themselves less dependent upon the once all-powerful princes, their employers of old. But they pay a high price for their freedom--they are forced to give lessons and public concerts, and hand over their compositions to publishers, simply to live. Still, their music is now out of the clutches of the aristocracy.

This family tree shows the evolution of music, young man. Just think! Men started by imitating us birds ... They've certainly made progress!

Tweet! Tweet!

It takes the son of a German Prince's lowly forest warden to give the opera a new lease on life. Christoph Willibald Gluck was born in 1714 in the Upper Palatine.

Gluck... before you leap

Italian opera is in a sorry state... now only an excuse for singers to show off. Gluck wants to restore the opera's lost dignity, so he simplifies the story-line and cuts any unnecessary ornamentation. "Orpheus and Eurydice" is his most famous work.

Gluck's operas are performed throughout Europe.

Gluck clashes with Piccini, the defender of the Italian tradition. The two composers join battle over the story of "Iphigénie en Tauride" ("Iphigenia on Tauris"). The "Gluckists" win the day... opera will now aim for simplicity and purity of line.

At the age of 8, Joseph Haydn enters the cathedral choir school in Vienna—until... his voice breaks... and his services are no longer required.

He works as a piano teacher... and as cellist for evening serenades...

An important turning point in Haydn's career comes with his appointment as choirmaster to Prince Esterhazy. The contract binding him to Esterhazy is extremely strict, but Haydn is not worried. A talented choir and orchestra are put at his disposal—for whom he will write religious music, operas, quartets—and half of his symphonies.

Haydn's music—in particular his quartets and symphonies—is a perfect example of the so-called "classical" genre...

His reputation grows... and his music is played everywhere in Europe. When Esterhazy dies, Haydn comes to London and is given a tremendous welcome. He is even asked to stay ... But—unlike Handel—he is not tempted.

Haydn is nicknamed "Papa" -- by all the musicians he helps—and also "The Father of the Symphony" -- because he had over 100 musical "offspring"!
One concert so excited the crowd that they mobbed the stage -- when a huge chandelier crashed onto the seats they'd just emptied! **No** one was hurt, so the symphony they'd heard became "The Miracle".
Joseph Haydn dies in 1809, the same year Napoleon invades Austria...

1789: The French Revolution: The great People's Uprising turns society upside down—music included! Vast choirs and orchestras become an important part of public ceremonies. This revolution deeply stirs the hearts and minds of the great composers of the early 19th century... They long for freedom...

Wolfgang Amadeus Mozart is the ultimate child prodigy—a brilliant musician who begins to compose at the age of 5 ... even before he can read or write!

For 10 years the young Wolfgang and his sister travel round Europe appearing in concerts organised by their father, Leopold, who was a shrewd businessman!

Mozart becomes the idol of Viennese high Society. Everyone is at his feet—including the family of the Emperor and Marie-Antoinette, the future Queen of France.

But Mozart returns to Salzburg—his birthplace—and enters the service of the Prince Archbishop. He composes both religious music...and serenades...

Mozart is enflamed with the new ideas of liberty and resents the archbishop's authority. After a somewhat heated discussion, he has to leave...

...for Vienna again...free indeed!

LE NOZZE DI FIGARO
DIE HOCHZEIT DES FIGARO
Eine comische Oper in
in Musik gesetzt
von
WOLFGANG AMADEUS MO
CLAVIER AUSZUG
HAMBURG

1782 sees the beginning of a happy life in Vienna where Mozart marries Constance. Commissions pour in... from the nobility, the wealthy bourgeois, from Emperor Joseph II himself...
Among the works composed during this period: the Mass in C, "The Abduction from the Seraglio", "The Marriage of Figaro".

Joseph II

51

Ludwig van Beethoven is both the first great Romantic and the last great composer of the Classical period. Born in Bonn in 1770, his childhood is unhappy. Beethoven's father, a hard and money-minded tenor, wants to exploit his son's talents — and makes him out to be a new Mozart. But Ludwig is not a child prodigy.

In Vienna, Austria, he is a pupil of "Papa" Haydn (*) who, along with Bach and Mozart, inspires his first compositions.

* see p. 48

To make ends meet, Beethoven gives piano lessons to the rich young ladies of Vienna. He is (understandably) appreciative of their (not only musical) talents...

ACH

1789: the French Revolution. Beethoven is fired by the new spirit of liberty which sweeps across Europe. In his symphonies and sonatas he begins to turn his back on tradition.

The Third Symphony — the "Eroica" — is written in honour of Napoleon Bonaparte. But when Napoleon is crowned emperor in 1804, when heroism turns into ambition, Beethoven scornfully tears up the dedication. This anger he will later translate into music.

52

The symphony is for Beethoven a means of translating feelings into music, of transforming sentiment into sound. The "Pastoral" Symphony – the Sixth – is a good example. Beethoven often composed as he walked in the country, and was familiar with the sounds of nature. But in the "Pastoral" he does more than to describe them he also communicates the feelings which his own description evokes. The music is both visual and emotional.

Great Scott, Nigel! Stereo grass!

This enforced solitude perhaps encourages his creativity -- his output is immense: 9 symphonies, 32 piano sonatas (written throughout his life), 2 masses, a violin concerto, 5 piano concertos, 16 quartets ...

Idiot! First, you are a few centuries late! Second, there are four in a quartet, not five! Third, your lyre is a little out of place. And last—but not least ....

But... tragedy strikes! Beethoven goes completely deaf. He'd never been one to seek the company of others. Now he is completely cut off from the world. To "converse" with his few friends Beethoven has to write everything down in a notebook.

... and one opera, "Fidelio": Leonore disguises herself as a jailer, "Fidelio", to save her husband, "Florestan", who has been unjustly imprisoned. The theme of the opera is close to Beethoven's heart: the triumph of justice and freedom over tyranny and oppression.

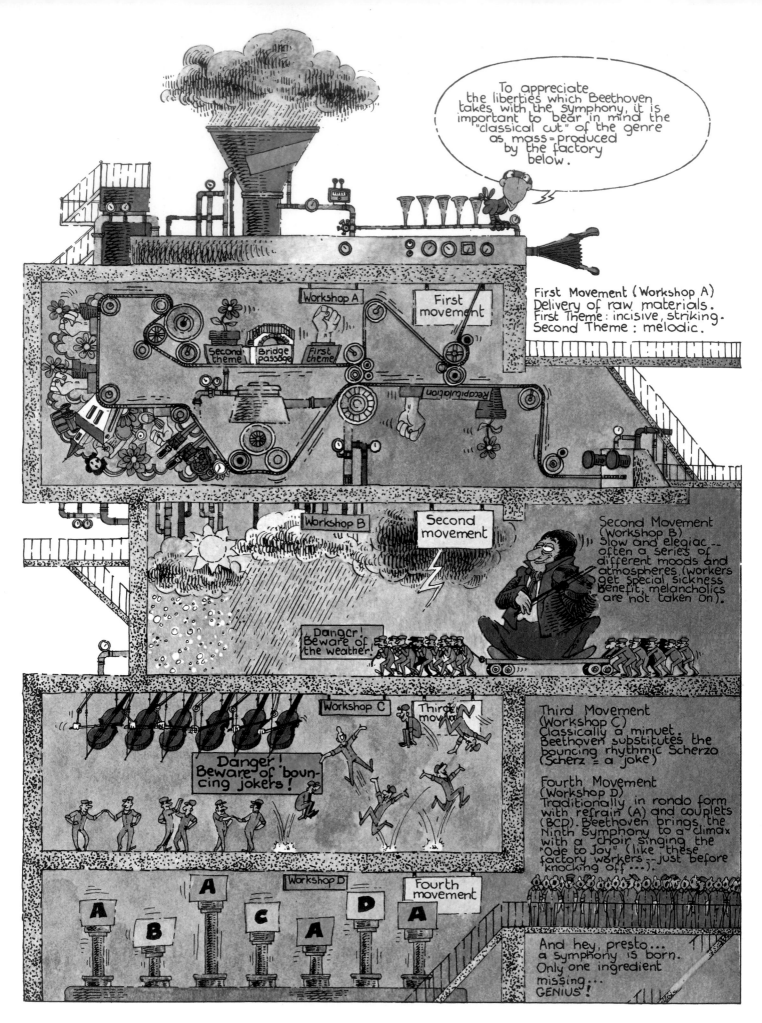

It is precisely Beethoven's genius that both the critics and the public find difficult to swallow. His ideas are too revolutionary and his last sonatas and quartets too difficult. Spontini and Weber—easier on the ear—are more popular.

And now listeners **scraaaaaatch** a moment of **pipipip** drama. Beethoven himself has just conducted choir and orchestra in a performance of his **scroooouutch** Ninth Symphony. The applause is deafening!! But... poor Beethoven can't hear it. A musician stands to tell the maestro to turn and take his bow **sssccccrrrrroouutchh.** (Please do not adjust your albums. There's just some bad weather over the century between us!)

Beethoven dies one evening in March 1827, lifting a defiant clenched fist to the heavens -- as a storm (in his honour?) breaks over Vienna.

30,000 people attend Beethoven's funeral.

Shortly afterwards a sad group of admirers meet up in a tavern...

Their idol is no more. Who will be the first among them to die? They drink a solemn toast to destiny's choice... It will be the young man in glasses... Franz Schubert.

Schubert is only 18 when he composes his famous song "Der Erlkönig" ("The Erl King"). Like his father, he scrapes a living as a schoolteacher, perhaps in order to get off military service, 15 years at the time! But music is his first love. The song tells of a child snatched away from the world of security and affection by a mysterious aristocrat from the Underworld...

Do us a favour, Erlkönig... Snatch me away from Mr. Schubert's lesson...

Schubert's name immediately evokes that of the Lied -- a poem sung to (most often) piano accompaniment. In his lyrical and dramatic Lieder Schubert marries text, melody and piano to perfection. But he also composes large-scale works: 10 sonatas, some 20 quartets, 9 symphonies, 5 operas and 6 masses...

Amen...

Aaaa-Schubert . . . .

1815: Napoleon is finally defeated at Waterloo. High hopes of liberty and revolution founder with him. The major powers meet at the Congress of Vienna. During the day they remake Europe...but during the evenings...they have a ball...

Aaaiiieee! Mind where you put your major powerful feet!!

It is here in Vienna that the waltz is taking its first tentative steps...The Strauss family (see page 84) are waiting in the wings...

Like Beethoven, Schubert likes to work in the country — where he finds peace and inspiration for "The Wanderer", "The Trout" and for the song cycle "Die schöne Müllerin" ("The Fair Maid of the Mill"). But if he likes to be by himself during the day...

...his evenings are less lonely! Music — no longer the prerogative of princes — is now made in cafés, restaurants and in the home of Dumpling's (Schubert's nickname!) Viennese friends. They feast on his music and Schubert...on his favourite dish - veal with cabbage! These evening parties are now called the "Schubertiads".

Of Schubert's nine symphonies, one of them — in b minor (1822) — has only two movements and is known as the "Unfinished". No one, until now, knew why. But at last the truth can be told! It is because Schubert....

But Schubert will never taste success outside the circle of his friends. He is not even able to find a full-time job as a musician. He sends his songs to Goethe. But the famous author is not impressed... Worse still, his publishers cheat him over "Die Winterreise" ("The Winter Journey"), paying him only $3 (£1.50) for 6 of the 24 songs!

Only $3! That's what I call being taken for a ride!

Schubert — like many Romantics — suffers from ill health. He is not only sensitive, he is also fragile... His music is often melancholy and resigned... In the andante movement of his string quartet in d minor he presents a series of variations on his song "Death and the Maiden"...

But death for Schubert is more than just a haunting theme... It is also a reality which constantly tracks him down. When he dies (of typhus) in November 1828 he is only 32"... The music he leaves us is both light-hearted and sad, at once profound and simple... a music capable both of expressing the depths of man's suffering.. and of singing... the beauty of the trout!

The Romantics adore the theatre.

The "inventor" of Romantic opera is Carl Maria von Weber. Weber's father runs a theatrical company and Karl's musical education is conducted "on the road".

His bohemian childhood marks him... He writes a song cycle called "The Power of Love and Wine" at the age of... 12 !!

Weber first makes a name for himself as a conductor. He is appointed musical director in Prague in 1813.

Weber seems to be the first conductor ever to use a baton...

...although contemporary engravings suggest the baton was more of a small stick.

Presto!

Piano, piano, if you don't mind!

His father—the Baron—is quite a character. One day he turns up at a rehearsal hoping to borrow some money from his famous son accompanied by his double bass and... two poodles!

Ma, non troppo

Allegro

In 1816 Weber moves to Dresden where he performs his operas "Der Freischütz" (1821) and "Euryanthe" (1825).

These are the very beginnings of German opera. In these lyric dramas melody is—at last—married to the dramatic language. Weber also employs the "leitmotiv"*, divides the opera into scenes and—big new idea!—uses the overture to create local colour and to announce the major themes of the drama to follow.

*A short, often repeated theme used to evoke a specific idea.

What a lovely drawing!

59

"Der Freischütz" is a huge success. The opera tells the story of a young marksman—Max—who, for love of the Beautiful Agatha, has a spell cast on his bullets... This magic story enthralls a whole generation of Romantic composers: Mendelssohn, Berlioz, Liszt, etc....

But in Paris, in order to pull in the crowds, the French tamper with the opera and turn it into a watered-down version of Robin Hood! The magic is lost...

Weber dies—of consumption—in London in 1826, seven weeks after the first night of his last opera, "Oberon". When his ashes are finally returned to Dresden in 1844, his funeral proves to be just as magical as his music. The coffin is carried above the heads of the crowd in a torchlight procession down to the banks of the Elbe, where it is placed on a boat transformed into a floating chapel... And who stage-managed this farewell extravaganza? A great admirer of Weber... one Richard Wagner (see p. 77).

Felix Mendelssohn is the odd Romantic out — being neither poor, unhappy nor rebellious!

Born in 1809 into a rich family of bankers, he is (literally) cushioned against life's hard edges... His father plays host to the intellectual elite of Berlin, among them Goethe, who is more encouraging to Felix than he was to Schubert...

Felix Mendelssohn 1809-1847

Mendelssohn shares the Romantic enthusiasm for Shakespeare. At the age of 17 he writes the overture to "A Midsummer Night's Dream" — to which he will later add the famous "Wedding March" — the music which has since led so many brides down the aisle and across the threshold of happiness...

Mendelssohn is also famous as a conductor. In March 1829 he conducts the "St. Matthew Passion" in the first performance since the death of Bach.

Mendelssohn composes for pleasure. His music is melodic and attractive — for instance, the 2 oratorios, the violin concerto, the 2 piano concertos and the five symphonies which include the gently exotic "Italian" and "Scotch".

Help!!

But if Mendelssohn is in some ways an exception... being a Romantic without excess... he cannot escape the tragic general rule... and dies young, at the age of 38, in March 1847.

Exactly what kind of piano is the mechanic (opposite) repairing? In the 18th century composers were still writing for the harpsichord, which works on a principle of plucked strings.

The piano does not come into its own until the 19th century. The strings are now struck by a hammer. The piano, with its vast expressive range and powerful sound, becomes the king of instruments. Piano building evolves slowly the age of the craftsman, eventually giving way to...

... the slick factory production of the 20th century.

A little boy reads the novels of Sir Walter Scott in his father's bookshop... Will he one day be an author? His father hopes so... But... a different future awaits Robert Schumann...

In 1828 – at the age of 18 – Schumann goes to study law in Leipzig, but the bar to which he longs to be called... is a musical one! He takes piano lessons with Frederick Wieck, one of whose daughters is both talented and pretty. Her name? Clara...

And now? The do-it-yourself Schumann portrait! Just cut along the dotted lines, assemble the bits and pop off to buy another copy of the book you've just ruined (joke!).

Schumann is ready to go to any lengths to become a virtuoso. He immobilises the middle finger of his right hand in order to strengthen the others. Result? The finger remains paralysed...

Schumann and his friends meet in the cafés of Leipzig. They publish a journal together -- in which Schumann defends his favorite composers: Bach and Beethoven.

In this revue Schumann compares Rossini to a canary.

At this rate we will end up comparing an eagle to Beethoven!!

Schumann signs his articles under two names: Eusebius and Florestan. The two reflect the two sides of his personality: the dreamer and the fanatic, the intellectual and the man of passion. We meet these two characters in his fresco for piano "Carnaval" (1834-1835).

Schumann does know some moments of peace – the "Forest Scenes", for instance – but such moments are rare and he and Clara Wieck live a hectic life.

"Much music was born of my struggles with Clara", he wrote – a kind of piano accompaniment to the dramatic silent movie of his life!

Robert and Clara fall in love (dainty tremolo)...

But (dramatic chord) Herr Wieck is opposed to their marriage. (Hissss)

Nonetheless, love will out. (Sigh)

In 1840 a court of law allows them to marry (Mendelssohn's "Wedding March").

That year Robert writes many songs and begins to make a name for himself.

Robert follows Clara on tour (gallop) -- travels which take them as far as ...

Russia! (Slavonic chords). Robert writes, Clara plays his compositions. He leaves Leipzig to conduct in Dresden ...

But remains unsatisfied, because misunderstood (weepy tune) ...

... and torn - he has to look after their 7 children! (weepy mo) fortissimo)

One ray of hope. Robert and Clara find happiness in Dusseldorf, where he conducts and composes his extraordinary Third Symphony ('The Rhenish). Sadly, although happy, this is not yet **THE END.**

Schumann's life is chaotic but he still composes a good deal: 4 symphonies, chamber music and many works for the piano.

Tragically he begins to develop grave psychological problems. He hears voices and talks to himself. In 1854 he seeks treatment in a clinic...

... only to escape the next day and throw himself in the Rhine! He is rescued from drowning but sent to an asylum - where he dies in 1859.

After Schumann's death Clara, his "Fidelio", travels all over Europe playing his music. "Pleasure and pain have always gone hand in hand", Schumann once wrote. Clara is assisted in her mission by one of Schumann's young admirers... Johannes Brahms (see p. 91).

Berlioz's problems are not only of the heart... The "Symphonie fantastique" is long – and musicians stop playing on the stroke of midnight. During one performance, they get up and leave before the end – leaving Berlioz (and the finale) to the faithful few remaining...

In 1834 the famous virtuoso Niccolò Paganini commissions "Harold in Italy" – Paganini himself playing Harold, the solo viola part. His technique is really incredible... Surely he must have more than five fingers on each hand...

Berlioz's religious music is a cure for unemployment! The "Requiem" (1837) calls for four brass bands and the "Te Deum" (1846) for full orchestra, organ and three choruses (a mere 600 choristers and 800 musicians!)

If Berlioz succeeds in filling the stage, he sadly empties the auditorium... "The Damnation of Faust", conducted by Berlioz himself at the Opéra Comique in Paris in 1846, receives a lukewarm press. One critic writes, "They might just as well have programmed an 'earthquake'"!!

Berlioz's one big popular success is his oratorio "L'Enfance du Christ" (The Childhood of Christ), written in 1855.

Berlioz had a fiery temperament, but Liszt is literally volcanic! Born in Hungary in 1811, he remains all his life a "mystical" Tzigane.

Liszt is yet another child prodigy. At the end of a concert Liszt gives in Vienna, Beethoven comes on stage to salute his talent, and Liszt is only 11!

Liszt is the Paganini of the keyboard. He revolutionises piano technique... when he plays, the instrument **explodes!**

But in 1823 Liszt is refused admission to the "Royal College of Music in Paris. The director, Cherubini, doesn't like child prodigies. No matter. Liszt soon makes a big hit in the "salons". And in the hearts of his admirers...

In 1835 Liszt meets his first "muse", Marie d'Agoult. It is in their beautiful house overlooking Lake Como that their second daughter is born. Cosima, the future wife of Richard Wagner.

Marie d'Agoult.

Liszt discovers new horizons for the piano...

and writes much for the instrument: a sonata, 19 Hungarian rhapsodies, 2 concertos, Concert Studies, Fantasies, Nocturnes -- and transcribes the works of other composers.

The piano has evolved mechanically -- thanks in particular to the work of Sebastian Erard -- and Liszt exploits to the full the new-found possibilities of volume, speed and colour.

Liszt gives concerts all over Europe. He is the first musician ever to give a "recital" – a concert featuring a single artist.

His music records his travels – for instance, the Swiss landscapes "Obermann's Valley", "By Lake Wallenstadt" and "Evening Bells" from the "Years of Pilgrimage".

But Liszt is by no means self-centred, and defends many young composers who have the reputation of being "difficult". He is wild in his applause of the "Symphonie fantastique" and personally conducts Wagner's "Flying Dutchman".

Liszt becomes a national hero. When he returns to Budapest in 1841 – where he founds an Academy of Music – he is welcomed by a torchlight procession of over 20,000 people and is presented with a sabre encrusted with precious stones.

Under the influence of Berlioz, Liszt turns to the symphonic poem – and will write 12 of them. In the famous "Dante Symphony" the architecture of the traditional symphony is abandoned – in favour of a more supple, organic form.

In the course of his life, Liszt tastes all the honours – both popular acclaim and professional esteem. But fame does not go to his head. Indeed, religion haunts both man and music. He writes a mass for the new cathedral at Gran in 1855, and the same year takes minor orders.

At Bayreuth in 1886 an ailing Abbé Liszt insists on going to a performance of Wagner's "Tristan and Isolde", and dies in the arms of his daughter Cosima.

In spite of Weber's success, the Italians are still top of the bill in the opera houses of Europe. Gioacchino Rossini soon outstrips all his rivals — including the jealous Spontini. Rossini's father wants his son to follow in his footsteps — he is the public health inspector of butcher shops in Pesaro in Italy! Rossini is none too keen...

...although his first opera is (ironically) butchered — with an amateur orchestra, second-hand sets and a leading soprano who can only sing one note in tune...

But success is just around the corner for the "Swan of Pesaro". At the age of 24 he writes "The Barber of Seville" in 15 days. A smash hit! And so begins a life full of banquets, bouquets and bravos...

O.K... so his music is a feast for the ears... but this?!!

Competition! Guess the titles of these Rossini operas. First prize? A pair of scissors for cutting out the portrait of Schumann...

Answer:
① The Silken Ladder. ② The Barber of Seville. ③ Cinderella. ④ The Thieving Magpie. ⑤ William Tell.

At the age of 37, having written some 40 operas, Rossini has reached the pinnacle of success. Why go on? Rossini decides to stop composing and in a symbolical gesture breaks his pen.

He gives himself over to other pleasures: travelling, doing nothing, cooking ...only composing... Some new dishes: cannelloni and the (in)famous Tournedos Rossini (steak with foie gras!) Towards the end of his life he once again abandons stove for stave, writing a "Stabat mater", the "Petite messe solennelle" and a series of witty, ironical piano pieces, such as "Oui les petits pois".

Destiny serves the last course of his life in 1868.

Bellini's brief life begins in Sicily in 1801. Success comes in 1827 at La Scala, Milan, with his opera "The Pirate". But Paris is the scene of the triumph of his three most famous operas: "La Sonnambula", "Norma" and "I Puritani" ("The Puritans").

Vincenzo Bellini (1801-1835).

"Norma" (1831) takes place during the struggle of the Druids against the invading Romans. Norma, a high priestess, vows the downfall of the Roman pro-consul with whom she was in love. Once he is condemned, Norma reveals the truth and perishes alongside him.

The Italian operas of this period are full of brilliant, florid show stoppers. This is the age of "bel canto" ("the beautiful song"). The orchestra is often reduced to playing the role of a huge guitar accompanying these lyrical jugglers!

When Bellini dies at the age of 34 Donizetti is left without a rival. He writes over 70 operas—all rich in melody—some comic: "The Elixir of Love", "Don Pasquale"; others tragic (the genre in which he excels): "Anna Bolena", "Lucrezia Borgia" and "Lucia di Lammermoor" (1835).

Gaetano Donizetti (1797-1848)

Is opera always so sad?

Quiet, please. An opera is a play entirely sung to the accompaniment of an orchestra. True, the subjects are often of a tragic nature. In France "opéra-comique" means an opera combining sung and spoken text (like "Carmen", p. 81), but the subject is not necessarily "comic". In fact, some "operas-comiques" are downright tragic!

"Lucia di Lammermoor" tells the tragic tale of two lovers separated by a family feud. Lucia loves Edgar, but is tricked into marrying Bucklaw. When she discovers the truth, she stabs her husband... and goes mad.

Donizetti himself is to share Lucia's fate, loosing his reason and dying in 1848.

In Venice, at the entry to the Biennale park, stand the busts of the two composers whose operas dominate the 19th century in Europe: Wagner and Verdi.

Verdi is born in Italy, in the province of Parma. His family are grocers, and he can only afford to study music thanks to a generous benefactor, Antonio Barezzi. But Verdi is not content just to be a country organist...

R. Wagner
1813 - 1883

G. Verdi
1813 - 1901

Merelli, the director of La Scala, commissions a comic opera from Verdi. But during the composition of "Un Giorno di Regno", tragedy strikes. His young wife and two children die in quick succession. On top of all this, the opera is a flop. Verdi vows never to compose again...

But Merelli will not let up and persuades Verdi to continue. Result? The triumph of "Nabucco" (1842). The Italians, who were living under the boot of the Austrians, find their patriotic pride, and nostalgia, poignantly expressed in the famous Hebrew chorus.

VA, PENSIERO

During this period Italy was divided into numerous small and independent states.

When the Italians revolt against the Austrians, Verdi is at the centre of the uprising. His very name is a rallying cry — calling for national unity! Vittorio Emmanuele Re D' Italia.

V.E.R.D.i

Italy once liberated, Verdi is elected to parliament.

In his best-known operas, "Rigoletto", "Il Trovatore", "La Traviata", Verdi transcends "bel canto", writing melodies which, although beautiful, also express the deepest and most complex emotions.

"Rigoletto" (1861) is based on a play by Victor Hugo. The hunchback jester Rigoletto serves in the court of the debauched Duke of Mantua. Destiny punishes him when he participates, unwittingly, in the murder of his daughter Gilda. It is not the body of the murdered duke which is in the sack he is dragging down to the river... but that of his own daughter.

"Ah, la maledizione!"

"Il Trovatore" (1853) — of Spanish origin — is a sombre tale of violence and jealousy. Leonora is in love with the troubadour Manrico. But the Count di Luna cannot contain his jealousy... He imprisons and finally executes Manrico... only to find that his rival was... his brother!

É spento! Egli era tuo fratello!

Ah! Io ritorno a vivere...

Love, death, jealousy. Jealousy, love, death... Opera? It's always the same old tune!...

"La Traviata" (1853) is based on Dumas' play "La Dame aux Camélias". Violetta, a "demi-mondaine", and the young Alfred Germont fall in love. For a while they are happy... but, to save the honour of the Germont family, Violetta must desert her beloved Alfred. When finally they are reunited... it is too late. The fragile Violetta dies in Alfred's arms.

Verdi's fame spreads far beyond the frontiers of Italy, and commissions pour in from abroad.

In 1865 the Imperial Theatre in St. Petersburg invites Verdi to compose a work for the people of Russia, and Verdi writes "La Forza del Destino" ("The Force of Destiny"). In order to direct rehearsals Verdi decides to brave the rigours of a Russian winter — and prudently takes a few Italian essentials along with him...

I've brought the subtitles for the Egyptian version.

In 1871 Verdi travels to Egypt, having written "Aida" to celebrate the opening of the Suez canal. "Aida" tells of the ill-fated love of an Egyptian soldier, Radames, for an Ethiopian slave girl, Aida. They are only to be united ... in death!

Towards the end of his life — and at the height of his glory — Verdi retires to his beautiful country house at Sant'Agata. But the "Old lion" has not had his last say. He is still to write two final works, which are the ultimate expression of his genius:

"Otello" (1887), based on Shakespeare's play, is yet another drama of jealousy, although the work is full of moments of great poetry .. such as the "Willow Song" sung by Desdemona in the final act.

"Falstaff" (1893), written when Verdi was 80, is also drawn from Shakespeare. The immense success of this truculent farce, which revolutionises traditional operatic forms, is final revenge for the failure of his first comic opera.

75

Popular German opera begins with Lortzing (1801-1864) whose work "The Carpenter-Tsar" tells the story of Tsar Peter the Great working incognito in a Dutch shipyard!

Flotow (1812-1883) has a big hit with "Martha" the adventures of an aristocratic lady employed as a serving girl -- her clumsiness soon reveals her noble origins!

Although Italian opera hogs the limelight throughout the 19th century, the lyric genius is nonetheless alive and well, and at work, in other countries...

Peter Cornelius (1824-1874) composes the extraordinary "Barber of Baghdad" -- the misadventures of a barber who falls in love with the Khalif's daughter.

Otto Nicolai (1810-1849) marries both Italian and German operatic styles in "The Merry Wives of Windsor".

At the beginning of the 19th century in France the fashion is for easy-going, gentle "operas-comiques". Inoffensive scores and stories, wedding-bell endings...

Major works are rare: "The White Lady" by F. Boieldieu (1775-1834), "Zampa" by F. Hérold (1791-1833), the ballet "Giselle" by A. Adam (1803-1856), whose 53 (!) operas have been somewhat forgotten...

...and "Mignon" by Ambroise Thomas (1811-1896) in which there is a big fire.

Mon sang se gla - ce !

Le feu ! Le feu !

Ironically -- and tragically -- the Opéra-Comique burns down one evening in 1887, during a performance of "Mignon". 400 people lose their lives!

As a result Monsieur Thomas is suspected of having "the evil eye"!

76

Finally, on stage, Richard Wagner... And what a character! Self-centred, beguiling, revolutionary, arrogant, and a musician of genius! His motto? "The world owes me all that I desire!" (1) His music is philosophical, dealing with the forces which rule the world. To this end he forges a union of poetry, music and theatre: Das Gesamtkunstwerk.

Poor and unknown, Wagner's early days in Paris are difficult. He is forced to sell the libretto of his opera "The Flying Dutchman" in order to pay his fare back home to Germany.

His reputation is first made in Dresden: with "Rienzi" (1842), "The Flying Dutchman" (1843) and "Tannhäuser" (1845) in which the hero arrives from the Venusberg to sing the joys of pagan love.

In 1848 both Europe and Wagner are fired by the revolutionary spirit! Indeed his activities worry the authorities...

...and Wagner goes to live with friends in Switzerland, but falls in love with the wife of his host! "Tristan and Isolde" (1859) is the result of this ill-fated passion, once having drunk the magic love potion the two lovers can only find happiness in death.

In a fairy=tale castle in Bavaria lives the young King Louis II, aesthete and patron of the arts. In 1864 he offers Wagner the use of his theatre. But the arrival of this ambitious careerist awakens deep jealousies, and Louis is forced to dismiss his new favorite...

Wagner returns to Switzerland, where he completes the Tetralogy (pp.   ). He is now living with Cosima, the daughter of Liszt. To celebrate the birth of their son Siegfried Wagner brings an orchestra into his house to play the dawn serenade, "The Siegfried Idyll" (1870).

Towards the end of his life his ambitious dream comes true. His own theatre is built on the sacred hill overlooking Bayreuth. This theatre, with its revolutionary acoustics (see plan), will be given over entirely to the performance of... the operas of Wagner!

The Tetralogy is a vast musical fresco which embodies both Wagner's musical and philosophical ideas. It is also known as the "Ring Cycle" ("Der Ring des Niebelungen"). The work is composed of four consecutive operas.

In "Das Rheingold" ("The Gold of the Rhine" 1869), Alberich the dwarf steals the precious ring, the treasure jealously guarded by the water sprites, which gives him total power over the world.

The ring is then again stolen by Wotan, King of the Gods...

...who passes it to two giants, Fasolt and Fafner, so that they can build the mighty Hall of Valhalla. The two giants quarrel and Fafner changes into a dragon.

In "Die Walküre" ("The Valkyries")(1870), Wotan once again seeks possession of the ring. He has two children and of their incestuous marriage Siegfried is born. Siegfried is the true hero, pure and good. Wotan is meanwhile forced to separate from his favorite daughter, Brunnhilde.

Brunnhilde is condemned to sleep forever on the summit of a mountain surrounded by flames. Only he who is oblivious of fear will be able to awaken her.

"Siegfried" (1876)—the valiant, the loyal, the innocent Siegfried—fashions a sword with which he kills Fafner and takes possession of the ring. A wood bird leads him to the mountain...

He passes through the circle of fire and arouses Brunnhilde from her deep sleep. Their mutual love promises for a brave, new world.

"Götterdämmerung" ("The Twilight of the Gods")(1876) dashes these hopes... Siegfried drinks a magic love potion which makes him forget Brunnhilde. Finally, he atones for his error, only to die. Brunnhilde on horseback throws herself onto Siegfried's funeral pyre.

Valhalla crumbles, the Rhine bursts its banks, the water sprites recover their precious ring... and the Reign of Man, the New Era, can now begin...

French opera with a truly French flavour is slow to emerge. During the reign of Napoléon III the stars are Halévy, Auber and Meyerbeer.

But their musical recipes are not very original... Auber's dishes come from Rossini's cookbook... And Meyerbeer serves up "bel canto" with a French dressing...

This "cuisine" is, however, much in favour - particularly when lavishly presented. The extravagant staging of Meyerbeer's "Robert le diable" and "The Huguenots" was only matched by ... the extravagant applause which greeted the final curtain.

The first truly French opera is written by Charles Gounod (1818-1893). Gounod was drawn to the church and studied theology for two years. His first compositions are religious (he is to write 15 masses!) and he signs his letters "Father Gounod".

But happily (for music!) Gounod, like Liszt, is equally attracted to the profane! He admires Berlioz and is inspired to write songs himself. His music inspired by the "Fables of La Fontaine" (including a two-act opera "La Colombe" in 1859) illustrates his supple gift for melody.

His luxurious tunes reflect the luxury of the period -- the plush Second Empire. Gounod is introduced to Napoléon III and, in the course of an outing, the Empress Eugénie herself comes up with an idea for a ballet...

In 1859 Gounod is 44. Until now his successes have been modest. Then suddenly "Faust" hits the jackpot.

The opera is one long string of delights: the "Soldiers' Chorus", the ballet, the "Jewel Song"...

Gounod's music, which is to influence Debussy, Fauré and Massenet, is essentially uncomplicated and its appeal immediate.

Ah, je ris de me voir si belle en ce miroir .... *

* "I feel pretty ... oh so pretty"...

French opera finally comes into its own with the work of a young composer, Georges Bizet. Bizet wins the Prix de Rome when he is 19... but this honour doesn't make him rich... In order to make ends meet, Bizet has to write cornet solos...

His teacher, Halévy, encourages him to write operas, and "The Pearl Fishers" (1863) and "The Fair Maid of Perth" (1867) are staged at the Paris Opera, but without much success.

The incidental music he composes for Daudet's play "L'Arlésienne" (1872) is only fully appreciated when played in its concert version by the famous conductor Pasdeloup (see p. 94).

Bizet's masterpiece is "Carmen", first staged at the Opéra Comique in 1875.

The quality and originality of the work are not immediately recognised — either by the public or by the performers. The ladies of the chorus don't think much of the idea of having to smoke and sing at the same time!

Don José, a soldier, falls in love with Carmen, a beautiful gypsy. Don José deserts to follow Carmen. But she, to taunt him, goes off with the matador Escamillo. Mad with jealousy, Don José tracks down and kills his beloved Carmen... just as the bullfight comes to a climax inside the arena...

Hell! Wrong frame!

Ah Carmen! Ma Carmen adorée.

Surprisingly, the opera is poorly received, although the philosopher Nietzsche (the friend of Wagner) considers the work to be the masterpiece of the "Latin genius".

Bizet, who suffers from a heart condition, is broken by the relative failure of "Carmen", and dies only three months after the opening night.

81

ars gallica

Saint-Saëns attempts to "nationalise" music! As president of the "Société Nationale de Musique" he declares himself against disorder and Wagnerian exaggeration and in favour of the essential French qualities (!) of logic, reason and clarity. As the Parnassians are to poetry, so Saint-Saëns is to music.

The search for national character is also to be found in instrumental music. In France four composers lead the way. First, the prolific Saint-Saëns: "I compose as naturally as an apple tree produces apples", he wrote.

The musical harvest is a good one! — 5 piano concertos, 3 violin concertos, 3 symphonies, chamber music and, especially, 4 symphonic poems which earn him the reputation of being the French Liszt. His art is well illustrated in the 14 short pieces composing "The Carnival of the Animals" (1886).

Keep your hair on, Samson!

I'm going to report this to the SPCMB* (society for the prevention of cruelty to musical birds)

Saint-Saëns also composes some 15 works for the stage, the most famous being the opera "Samson and Delilah".

Just before his death in 1921 Saint-Saëns writes the first film music ever, which he records on a piano roll.

Leo Delibes 1836-1891

Leo Delibes also seeks to compose an essentially French music. He is well known for his operettas and, "opéras-comiques"—, "Lakmé" (1885). He is the inventor of a new genre: the symphonic ballet.
"Coppelia" is one of the tales of Hoffmann. Frantz falls in love with Coppelia, a mechanical doll, built by the old craftsman, Coppelius. But when he discovers the truth, Frantz returns to his real-life fiancée.

82

And now, Ladies and Gentlemen, for a little light refreshment... What better antidote to all these dramas than... a sparkling dash of operetta.*

The moving spirit of operetta was born in Cologne in 1819... but Offenbach's father has the good sense to bring his son to Paris, where he becomes, according to Rossini, the "Mozart of the Champs Elysées"!!

Offenbach is first employed as conductor/composer at the "Comédie Française". "Orpheus in the Underworld" (1858) heralds a string of easygoing, joyful operettas which make Offenbach a creator in his own right: "La belle Hélène" (1864), "La vie parisienne" (1866), etc...

* An opera based on a light, fanciful story.

But in 1870 France is plunged into the civil war of "The Commune". This is no time for gaiety... and Offenbach himself tolls the knell of "La Belle Époque" with his one opera and masterpiece, "The Tales of Hoffmann".

Offenbach dies in 1880 — and with him disappears forever a certain kind of privileged "joie de vivre".

Offenbach (1819-1880)

Jules Massenet (1842-1912)

Ah! Pitié! Grace
je ne veux pas!..

Charlotte, je meurs...

But the Romantic spirit is still alive... At the end of the century Massenet, in his operas "Manon" (1884) and "Werther" (1892), once again plunges us into an emotional world of passion and despair.

Werther, in the grip of an impossible love, commits suicide. Charlotte arrives... only to find her beloved at death's door...

Meanwhile... back in Vienna ... they're still dancing (guess what?) the **WALTZ**! The craze sweeps the whole country. Everyone is waltzmad. Every night over 50,000 dancers one-two-three around the huge, glittering dance halls.

The waltz becomes an art form, thanks to Joseph Lanner (1801-1843) and, especially, to the Strauss family.

Johann, the founder of the musical dynasty, trains to be a bookbinder, but throws it all in for music. He often plays at court balls. One evening, unhappy with the sound coming out of his fiddle, he pours beer into it (= mus-hic?)

Johann has three sons: Joseph, Edward and Johann Junior, the brilliant composer who will bring glory to the whole family.

Johann, Jr., is not content to write simple waltzes—he adds slow introductions, reprises, sumptuous melodies...

It is Johann, Jr., who pens the most famous of all Viennese waltzes—"The Blue Danube". When he first heard it, Brahms exclaimed with envy: "How I wish I'd written that!"

JOHANN STRAUSS II

Johann, Jr., writes over 500 waltzes, polkas, quadrilles and galops. In his famous operetta "Die Fledermaus" ("The Bat", 1874), he paints a picture of frivolous Viennese society towards the turn of the century.

The revival of Scandinavian music begins with the Swedish composer Franz Berwald. But it is in Norway, in the music of Edvard Grieg, that the most determined reaction against Wagner and Romanticism is to be heard.
Grieg turns to Norwegian folk music for inspiration.

Grieg takes himself off to a shack overlooking the Troldhaugen (the "Fairy Mountain") and composes music which will enchant the whole of Europe: 3 violin sonatas, the "Norwegian Dances", a piano concerto, and, especially, the incidental music for Ibsen's play "Peer Gynt". This score, with its trolls, its mists and its mountains, is full of Scandinavian folklore. It opens — a symbol of a national musical awakening? — with the famous passage "Morning Mood".

It's the latest Grieg!

Here! I know that tune!

Phew! And here I am, just in time to announce another (somewhat early) national awakening (and now back to beá!).

Edvard Grieg 1843-1907

Over a long period the Czechs had imported their music and musicians. Smetana is the first to compose in the national colours... although he is influenced by Liszt and Wagner.

MOZART
WEBER
BERLIOZ

Bedrich Smetana (1824-1884)

Smetana is born into a musical family and plays the violin part in a quartet at the age of 6. His music is deeply patriotic, as is his life, he serves in the national guard during the 1848 uprisings. The symphonic cycle "My Country" (1874) and the opera "The Bartered Bride" are both steeped in Bohemian folklore and capture the very essence of his country.

Ever since the time of Peter the Great, Russia has depended upon musical imports from the West. This one-way traffic hinders the development of Russian music.

Glinka (1804-1898)

Glinka—born in 1804—is the Grand Old Man of Russian music. Born into the well-to-do nobility, Glinka can afford to travel. In France he discovers the castles of the Loire Valley and ... the cuisine!

FRAGILE
FRAGILE
FOREIGN MUSICIAN
TOP

The overture to his famous opera "A Life for the Tsar" (1836) is a panorama of Russian folk songs and dances.

Glinka's initiative inspires the Five—all amateur musicians—who will carry on his work.

First, Balakirev (1837-1910): an able teacher and a good musician, but who writes little: 2 symphonies, a symphonic poem "Thamar" (1867), an Oriental fantasy for piano, "Islamey" (1869) and many songs.

Balakirev is a strange man. A fortuneteller decides the programmes for his concerts...

...which draw few people—only 10 in St. Petersburg in 1872...

For 5 years, he works in the ticket office of a Russian railway station...

And then becomes a mystic, living surrounded by animals, only eating fish...

The second member of the Five is César Cui (1831-1918). He is a military engineer, an expert in fortifications. But music penetrates his defences. He writes songs, chamber music and 10 operas. His theoretical writings are a manifesto of the Five.

Cooooeeee César

The third member of the Five is Alexander Borodin (1854-1887)—who wants to be a surgeon, but tends to pass out! He becomes a chemistry teacher instead. A generous man, always helping others, he has little time for music.

Borodin's best-known work is his opera "Prince Igor"—which tells the story of the struggles between the Russians and the Polovtsy—the nomadic invaders of the 12th century.
He also writes 3 symphonies, 2 quartets and an orchestral "picture", "In the Steppes of Central Asia" (1880).

This little boy who is listening to his nurse tell of old Russian legends will be the fourth member of the group.

Modeste Mussorgsky (1835-1881) will not forget these stories. His greatest work "Boris Godunov" (1869), tells of the coming to power of the regent after the death of Ivan the Terrible. There are many crowd scenes in the opera. "I want to put the Russian people on stage", he wrote.

This sympathy for the down-trodden associates Mussorgsky with other artists: Tolstoy, Gogol and Turgenev, for instance. His own life is full of unhappiness. He resigns from the army to compose... but finds himself penniless...

Mussorgsky's muscular, rhythmic music is also very "visual". The "Pictures from an Exhibition" (1874) record his impressions of the works of an artist friend. Originally for the piano, this work will be orchestrated in 1922 by the pensive spectator below, Maurice Ravel.

...the "Capriccio Espagnol" (1887) and the symphonic suite "Scheherazade" (1888): the sultan believes all women to be unfaithful and decides to do away with his wives! But Scheherazade enthralls him with her story, which lasts the required 1001 nights — and thus saves her life!

The last member of the Five is Nikolai Rimsky-Korsakov (1844-1908). First a naval officer, he becomes a teacher at the St. Petersburg Conservatory in 1871. Stravinsky will be one of his pupils.

He writes several operas and also orchestral music coloured by the styles of different countries and different periods: "The Russian Easter Festival Overture" (1888)...

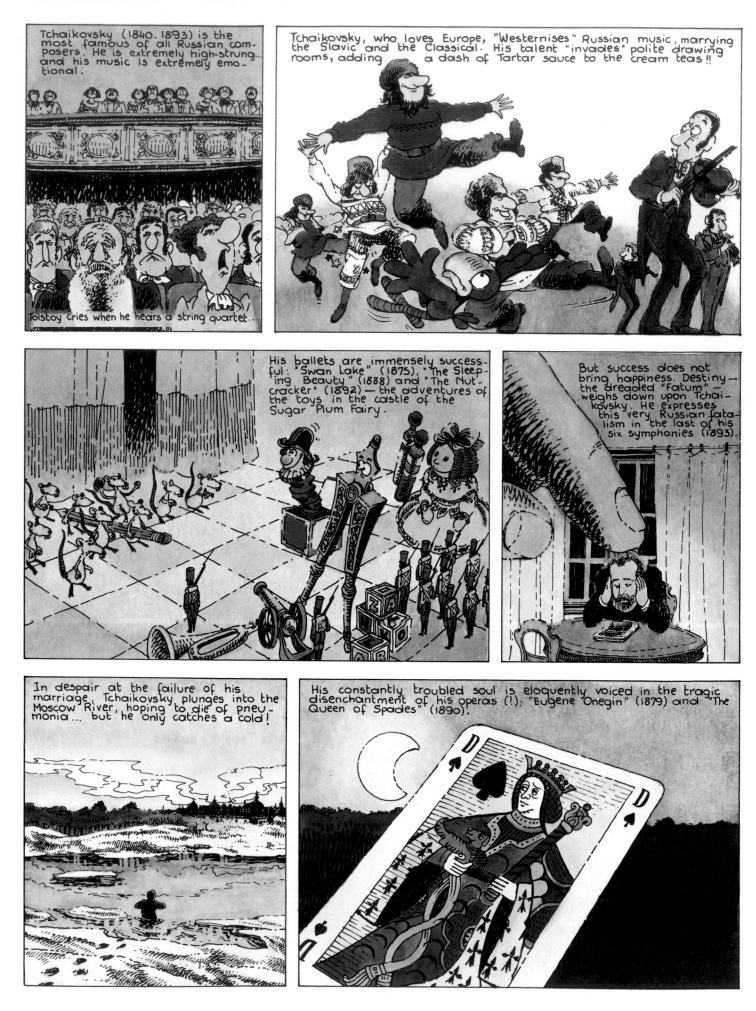

Tchaikovsky (1840-1893) is the most famous of all Russian composers. He is extremely high-strung... and his music is extremely emotional.

Tolstoy cries when he hears a string quartet...

Tchaikovsky, who loves Europe, "Westernises" Russian music, marrying the Slavic and the Classical. His talent "invades" polite drawing rooms, adding a dash of Tartar sauce to the cream teas!!

His ballets are immensely successful: "Swan Lake" (1875), "The Sleeping Beauty" (1888) and "The Nutcracker" (1892) — the adventures of the toys in the castle of the Sugar Plum Fairy.

But success does not bring happiness. Destiny — the dreaded "Fatum" — weighs down upon Tchaikovsky. He expresses this very Russian fatalism in the last of his six symphonies (1893).

In despair at the failure of his marriage, Tchaikovsky plunges into the Moscow River, hoping to die of pneumonia... but he only catches a cold!

His constantly troubled soul is eloquently voiced in the tragic disenchantment of his operas (!): "Eugene Onegin" (1879) and "The Queen of Spades" (1890).

90

The increasing importance of this new musical nationalism does not mean that Beethoven has been forgotten. His influence is at work in the brilliant German "school": Brahms, Bruckner and Mahler.

In 1863, when he is 20, Brahms leaves his native Hamburg to tour as accompanist to the famous gypsy violinist Reményi.

Brahms's talents as a composer are discovered by...Robert Schumann, who praises him to the skies in his journal: "At last Brahms arrives...bringing new blood to music".
After Schumann's death, Brahms becomes the close companion of Clara.

Not for Brahms the excesses of Romanticism. His music expresses highly charged emotions — but in supple, traditional forms. He is a quiet, serious, even solitary man — with a penchant for the melancholic sound of the French horn...

"J'aime le son du cor, le soir, au fond des bois..."
-Verlaine-

Brahms adores children, and his pockets (like his music!) are always full of sweet things...

He lives as a professional musician, but when he fails to become a conductor in Hamburg, Brahms moves to Vienna...

...where, every day at the stroke of 12, he is to be seen in the tavern, which still exists, "Zur Roten Igl" ("The Red Eagle"). Success comes in 1868 with the "German Requiem", written in memory of Schumann.
Brahms also writes 4 symphonies, 2 piano concertos, the famous violin concerto and a series of sumptuous chamber works...

...and almost 200 Lieder. His symphonies tend to express the conflict of grand ideas, but his songs are intimate and personal...Mothers the world over still sing their children to sleep with his (resist it if you can!) "Lullaby"...

91

In 1860 Brahms lends his name to a petition which protests against the "New Music". And so German music finds itself divided—Brahms, the Classical composer, pitted against Bruckner, the Wagnerian.

TRADITION   AVANT-GARDE

Bruckner is brought up in an atmosphere of sacred music and his own compositions are naïvely, fervently religious. Indeed, he is nicknamed "The Minstrel of God"!

Bruckner is an extremely humble man. In 1865, at the late age of 31, he takes up his musical studies again, and continues for the next 5 years!

His life and music are completely changed when he discovers Wagner's luxurious chromatism*.

(*musical colouring.)

Like Beethoven, Schubert, Dvorak and later Mahler, Bruckner also writes nine symphonies — the fatal number?! His works are often vast: huge orchestras, lengthy scores. Brahms calls them "python symphonies" — they just never seem to stop unfurling...

Bruckner also writes motets, 3 masses, and a Te Deum. For him the orchestra is like a giant organ playing to the glory of God.

His last wish? To marry faith and music, and to be buried under the organ of the church of St. Florian in Austria.

At 9 o'clock every morning in Paris during the 1860's a quiet-looking man slips unnoticed into the church of St. Clotilde. Who is he? None other than César Franck, the famous organist and one of the most remarkable composers of his generation.

Franck is also a teacher. He and his pupils form a "school", "Le Franckisme", in reaction against gimmicky, modish music. Franck's own compositions are intense and passionate — as in the oratorios, the symphonic poems "Le chasseur maudit" (1882), "Les Djinns" (1884) and in the elegant, imposing Symphony in D minor (1888).

His chamber music is equally moving — and his violin sonata haunts Marcel Proust... but not, sadly, Madame Franck, who, to her husband's dismay, does not appreciate his music...

Franck takes refuge in St. Clotilde, where he plays on an organ built by Cavaillé-Coll.

His pupil Vincent d'Indy writes: "It was in that dark organ loft that Franck spent the best part of his life..."

The fourth composer to promote this French musical renaissance is Edouard Lalo, but his music is so discreet that it remained unknown for a long time.

Lalo is a musical "colourist" a talent revealed in his Breton opera, "Le Roi d'Ys" (1879), his "Spanish Symphony" (1874) and his "Norwegian Rhapsody" (1881).

This new-style French music is played at the Pasdeloup concerts, which are held in the Cirque d'Hiver in Paris (The Winter Circus Hall).

Meantime, at the Niedermeyer School, young French musicians are being trained—14 pianos all in the same room from 7 in the morning to 11 at night!! Extraordinary that a musician as discreet as Fauré (see p.) should emerge unscathed from this pandemonium!

Towards the end of the century the nationalistic fervour begins to die down. Emmanuel Chabrier, a witty civil servant with a taste for music, is 100% pure Wagnerian — but, an odd mixture!... he manages to keep his French sense of humour.

Chabrier is a close friend of the Impressionist painters — and is here to be seen "At the Piano" in the famous painting by Fantin-Latour.

His instrumental music is airy, brilliant and full of spirit. Listen, for example, to "España". One impressionist that will be influenced by Chabrier is Maurice Ravel.

That, Emmanuel!! He just tickles my keys... Tee=hee!!

The influence of both Franck and Wagner is to be felt in the music of Ernest Chausson. Debussy looked on him as an "elder brother" and much admired his "Poem for Violin and Orchestra" (1896). The famous Belgian violinist Eugène Ysaÿe is here playing the work dedicated to him.

Chausson's refined music is to be heard in his "Symphony in B flat major" (1890) and in his "Poème de l'amour et de la mer" for voice and piano (1882).

Chausson's career is tragically brief. One day in the midst of writing a scherzo, he decides to take a ride on his bicycle, falls, and cracks his skull against a wall...

94

These operas express the spirit of the "Belle Epoque" -- their brilliant changing colours revealing glimpses of a profound psychological malaise.

Freud -- the father of psychoanalysis, is lurking in the wings. His first works are published at the time of "Salome".

After the end of the First World War, Strauss pursues his career as conductor of the Vienna State Opera. He continues to write lavish and sophisticated operas, such as "Ariadne auf Naxos" (1912) -- composed originally as an entertainment to accompany Molière's play "Le Bour- geois Gentilhomme".

Strauss will not die until 1949 -, we shall meet him again later.

The tradition of the Lied is continued in the work of Hugo Wolf -- who writes 232 songs, including several song cycles.

Each Lied is an opera in miniature.

"Even small things can be enchanting".*

At times his music is serene and optimistic.

* From the "Italian Song-Book" (1891).

... at other times it expresses his disturbed psychological condition.

At the end of his life Wolf sinks into madness.

Like Liszt, whom he often plays, Busoni (1866-1924) is a virtuoso of the keyboard! He gives concerts of all the great Romantic composers ...

According to Diaghilev,* this is the beginning of "nasty" music!

* see page 109.

... But in his theoretical writings and in his own music he is anti-Romanticism. He doesn't seek to create "nice sensations". For him the piano is a percussion instrument! His most famous work is his opera "Doktor Faust".

Alban Berg is a pupil... and disciple... of Schoenberg. At the same time, Berg remains attached to Romanticism. His atonal music is deeply personal and lyrical. He writes two great operas based on stark, brutal stories.

"Wozzeck" (1921) tells of a dull-witted soldier who discovers that the woman he loves is having an affair with the drum-major. He stabs her and then drowns in the lake...

"Lulu" (1934) is about a beautiful woman who kills her "protector", only to fall under the knife of... Jack the Ripper.

The violin concerto, "In Memory of an Angel", is dedicated to a young girl who died when she was 18. The music is a marriage of the tonal and the atonal.

The concerto is also Berg's last work. He dies in 1935 as the result of an insect bite!... just before penicillin became readily available.

The third founder/composer of the new Viennese school is Anton Webern. His music is more difficult, more cerebral than that of Berg. He writes only about 30 scores...

... some of which don't last long! The shortest? About twenty seconds!

Phew! I'm late. Have they started?

Started? They've just fi-nished!

Webern is a modest man, but Boulez says of him: "His place is unique in contemporary music". In Austria he conducts music played and written by the workers...

VIVA WEBERN

His end is tragic. In 1945 he is shot in error by an American soldier on duty outside his house. He had come out to smoke a cigar.

French opera also goes through a "Realist" stage. Massenet (see page 83)-- whose music influences Puccini and Debussy--continues to wallow in heroic, romantic subjects: "Thaïs" "Werther", "Manon", "Le Cid". But Charpentier brings things down to earth with "Louise" (1900).

Louise's father, a plumber, is opposed to her marriage to the poet Julian. Debussy couldn't stand the "tuneful" nature of this opera!

Hardly the stamp of genius?

The "tuneful" -- but subtle! -- Fauré turns away from Realism.

A modest and extremely honest man, the poor Fauré is cheated by his publisher!

Fauré is a poet who translates into music the serene and melancholic dreams of Verlaine's "Fêtes galantes".

The musician Fauré and the poet Verlaine are both inspired by the world of the 18th-century artist Watteau.

It is Fauré's chamber music which first brings him to public notice. His "Requiem" (1887) makes him famous.

The opera "Penelope" is a fine example of his talent. Patient and faithful, Penelope doesn't recognise Ulysses when he returns at last, disguised as a beggar...

And now, Ladies and Gentlemen ... the Parade of the New Style National Composers!

The growing importance of this musical nationalism is in part due to a reaction against the influence of Germany.

First Russia... and Prokofiev.

Stravinsky's music is international; Prokofiev's music reflects more closely the spirit of his country.

But like Stravinsky, his first works are aggressive, dissonant, even brutal. The "Scythian Suite" provokes a scandal in St. Petersburg in 1916.

The violence of his music mirrors the violence of the Russian Revolution in 1917.

But his music can also be tender... "The Love for Three Oranges" (1919) is light and melodious...

Prokofiev travels a lot, but never stops writing -- "Romeo and Juliet", "Lieutenant Kijé", "Peter and the Wolf", as well as symphonies and concertos... He even composes on the train.

In 1934 he returns to Russia for good -- offering his talent to the service of the People...

Help!

Sssshhhhh, please! Eisenstein is shooting the famous Battle on the Ice from the film "Alexander Nevsky" -- for which Prokofiev writes the music.

Bartok has one domineering passion -- the music of his native Hungary. And one over-riding fear -- for the future of Humanity. These two obsessions characterize his music.

The "Cantata Profana" (1926) -- for soloists, augmented orchestra and chorus -- is taken from a Hungarian legend which tells of a huntsman and his three sons who are changed into stags (a deer price to pay!)

Bartok is deeply distressed by the ugliness and brutality of the world. His quartets and his "Music for Strings, Percussion and Celesta" (1936) are masterpieces born of his anguish.

Bartok's fears are justified. World War II erupts. Hitler over-runs Europe ... and the world is menaced ...

Bartok takes refuge in the USA. But he hasn't enough money to live on ...

In spite of his penury he writes the extraordinary "Concerto for Orchestra" (1943), a showpiece for his instrumental genius.

Bartok dies of leukemia in 1945. Poor, as yet unknown to the American public, he leaves his Third Concerto for Piano unfinished ...

With his fellow composer Zoltan Kodaly, Bartok publishes collections of traditional folk music.

Hungarian Folk Songs
1906

Bartok Kodaly

Kodaly's music is less ambitious than that of Bartok, and its popular origins more easily recognizable.

The comic opera "Hary Janos" (1926) tells of the adventures of a boastful old soldier, who fights Napoleon and (of course...) wins!

After the death of Purcell (see p. 39) Great Britain crosses a musical desert...

Music... my kingdom for a drop of music... AAAHHH

Queen Victoria has the reputation for being narrow-minded, but during her reign music starts to blossom again.

This is the period of the famous choral societies...

... and of the Doyly-Carte Opera Company, which puts on the bouncing, tongue-twisting operettas of Sir Arthur Sullivan and his librettist, W. S. Gilbert.

In "Iolanthe" (1882), Sullivan writes a chorus for fairies... who are some- what past their prime!

Music celebrates both the beauty of the countryside and the imperial aspirations of Victorian Great Britain...

Delius is the poet of the countryside: "The English Meadow", "Brigg Fair", "A Village Romeo and Juliet"...

But Edward Elgar extols the glory of the British Empire in his triumphant marches "Pomp and Circumstance".

Oh! To be in England...

However British in spirit, Elgar betrays the influence of Wagner and Mahler in his famous "Enigma Variations".

Gustav Holst's popular orchestral suite "The Planets" (1916) is likewise inspired by European music.

I thought we spheres were supposed to make harmonious music!

MARS

Seeking to create a music that is more genuinely British in inspiration, Ralph Vaughan Williams turns to folk songs...

... and, even, to the sounds of London itself in his Second Symphony (1913)...

The Seventh Symphony pays tribute to the bravery of the explorer Scott and his companions in the icy wastes of the Antarctic...

Excuse me, gentlemen. Which way to the Pole, please?

The greatest British composer of the century is perhaps Benjamin Britten. His gifts are most apparent in his operas...

... such as "Peter Grimes" (1945), the tragedy of a lone fisherman, shunned by his community, whom the village school mistress vainly tries to save...

To each tragedy its music... The "War Requiem" is born of Britten's abhorrence of war.

At other times his music sensitively translates the workings of love...

"The Turn of the Screw" is based on a story by Henry James. The ghost of an evil servant holds two children in its spell.

Britten also writes joyful, light-hearted music for children, such as the "Young Person's Guide to the Orchestra" and the "Ceremony of Carols".

Have you got enough change, Arthur? There must be at least three of them...

"Si-i-i-lent Night, Ho-o-o-oly Night. All is calm, all is bright..." Thanks, Arthur!

KOZY KOT

Two other composers are prime movers in this New Spanish Renaissance: Turina, who writes the famous "La Oración del torero" (The Bull-fighter's Prayer)...

... and Rodrigo, composer of the world-famous "Concierto de Aranjuez" for guitar and orchestra.

Hasta la vista!

And now we head for South America... Passports ready!

...where we arrive in Brazil, home of Heitor Villa-Lobos. In the opera houses and in the lush drawing rooms of the rich, European music still holds sway...

... But in the streets, you can dance to another kind of music, a music which casts a spell over the little Heitor.

Villa-Lobos travels into remote northern Brazil to record the songs of the natives.

In order to develop musical education, he encourages choral singing on a massive scale. One day, from high up on a tower, he conducts 40,000 people!

Pass the binoculars. I can't see his arms...

The music of Villa-Lobos is the very image of his country. It is a mixture of the genuine Brazilian and of the traditional European, as in "The Amazon", the "Discovery of Brazil" and in the famous "Bachianas Brasileiras", which are inspired by the music of Bach.

ELDORADO

Step This Way For North America.

123

126

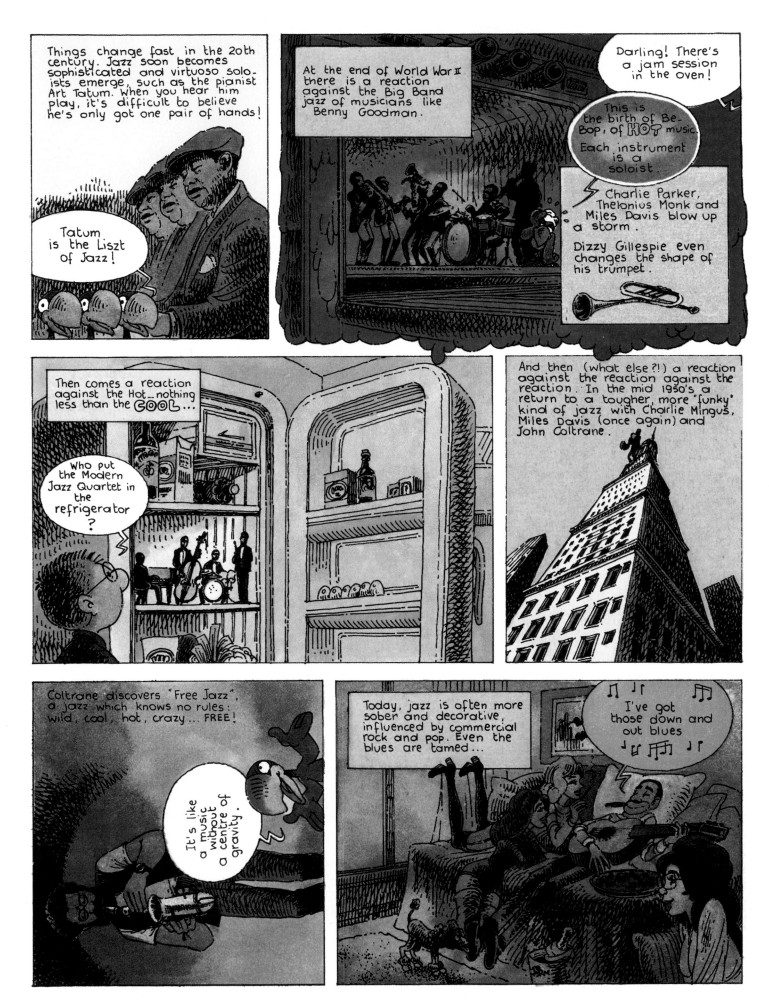

127

130

133

Boulez's first big success is "Le Marteau sans maître" -- a work which combines the styles of Debussy, Webern, the Balinese Game-lang and traditional Japanese music!

His music causes a sensation! "Polyphony X" (1951) which is 100% serial, is physically unbearable!

"Doubles" (1956), which explores sound in space, requires a long and complicated re-arrangement of the orchestra...

Boulez admires the poet Mallarmé who, scornful of everyday communication, seeks a New Language.

After "Pli selon Pli" (1958-1960), which is inspired by Mallarmé, Boulez leaves France to concen-trate on his career as a conductor. He conducts a triumphant "Ring" at Bayreuth...

Leading light number 2: Stock-hausen, whose first works, the "Klavierstücke" and "Kontra-punkte", are examples of serial music.

But with "Gruppen" for three orchestras (!), he moves away from serial music to explore music in space...

Knotty problem for the conductors of "Gruppen".

Then... a revelation! Stockhausen discovers music on tape, and writes "Gesang der Jünglinge" (1956) ("Song of the Young Men"), which marries taped "musique concrète" and electronic music.

Sigh...

The pioneers of "musique con-crète" are Pierre Schaeffer and his team in Paris. "Musique con-crète" is composed of recorded sound taken from life -- for example, "Variations for a Door and a Sigh" (1963) by Pierre Henry.

Electronic music, on the other hand, is made of sounds created by a machine.

Pierre Henry also seeks to make music from the waves emitted by the brain!

Is this a brain operation?

No. It's a concert.

In 1967 Stock-hausen writes his "Hymnen", a series of electron-ic variations on national anthems!

A Some-what uncom-mon musical experience!

Help! Mayday!

134

The third big name in modern music is that of the Italian Luigi Nono. He marries Schoenberg's daughter and espouses very left-wing ideas!

"For me, making music and protesting in the streets are one and the same thing".

Nono composes many works for the voice.

"Il canto sospeso" is inspired by letters written by Resistance fighters condemned to death.

Revolt against political and social injustice is the basis for much of his work, for example, the opera "Intolerance" and "The Illuminated Factory", for voice and tape.

Luigi Dallapiccola, like his compatriot Nono, also endeavours to write "humanitarian" music, and composes many vocal works.

"Night Flight" (1939), based on the work of the French author Saint-Exupéry, is at once lyrical and dodecaphonic. This opera is a hymn to man's heroism.

Dallapiccola uses prison as an image of injustice _ in "Prison Songs" (1941) and the opera "The Prisoner" (1948).

Then in the we ...

Although we are well into the experimental period, don't forget that "orthodox" classical music is still being written! In 1948, a year before his death, Richard Strauss composes his exquisite "Four Last Songs".

Nonetheless ... the evolution of contemporary music is closely linked to the search for New Sounds. Composers no longer endeavour to portray happiness or sorrow, joy or despair, they compose to invent and innovate. Their innovations are sometimes ... surprising?!

John Cage, for instance, distorts the sound of the piano by putting nuts, bolts, screws and bits of wood in the works!

Cage's music is a cocktail of Zen, practical jokes and brilliant new ideas! One of his works is composed for all the "instruments" to be found in a living room: chairs, tables, etc.

"4'33"" or the "Silent Sonata" is simply the sound made by the audience during the 4 minutes 33 seconds that the pianist spends on stage... without playing a note! The audience becomes the soloist!

135

A similar kind of musical anarchy is practised by the Argentinian composer Mauricio Kagel. Kagel is a clown in sound! This is the "Music of the Absurd"!

"Match" is a game of tennis for two cellos...

Less extravagant, more intellectual is the music of André Boucourechliev, who explores the possibilities of aleatory music (see Ives, p. 124).

In "Archipelagos" the performers "navigate" their passage through the score, avoiding collisions and tonal pollution!

Yet another new departure... repetitive music! Two Americans, Steve Reich and Terry Riley, both influenced by pop and by Oriental music, write hypnotic, trance-inducing music!

ZZZZ

Each composer goes his own way, does his own thing! Xenakis, a pupil of the architect Le Corbusier, creates extraordinary sound structures: "Nights", which is dedicated to political prisoners the world over; "Terretktorh", in which the orchestra is situated in the audience...

...and the famous "Polytope de Cluny", a pageant of light and sound presented in the ancient Hôtel des Abbés de Cluny in the centre of Paris.

The Italian Luciano Berio draws inspiration from the literary works of Proust and James Joyce and invents musical "collage".

Hans Werner Henze composes in two styles. The opera "Boulevard Solitude" (taken from the 18th century French novel "Manon Lescaut") is dodecaphonic. "The Stag King" and the ballet "Ondine" are situated on the frontiers of "tonality". In both styles Henze triumphs...

Index